Beginner's Gu Shu.

by Wilburt Mayo

1. What Is Feng Shui?

Feng Shui (pronounced fung shway) is an ancient Chinese practice that involves art and science. It has been around for thousands of years. The practice relies on the laws of heaven and earth to help people balance their energies within a space. This is to help them receive fortune and health.

The word "feng" means wind and "shui" means water. Therefore Feng Shui means "wind water". The local Chinese people place wind that is gentle and water that is clear in one setting. It is to represent good health and harvest.

Feng Shui prides itself on thinking that the land includes Chi. The work Chi has to do with energy. Back in ancient times, the local Chinese people claimed that the energy of the land would be good or bad for others.

Feng Shui comes from the Taoist ideals in order to deal with nature. Taoism deals with religious and philosophical beliefs. Taoism has a strong influence in Asia.

Taoism is also responsible for birthing yin and yang concepts. Yin and yang deal with opposite aspects of a phenomenon or comparing two phenomena. They represent quality in regard to correspondence which is found in most areas of Chinese science and philosophy. An example of this would be ancient Chinese medicine.

In addition to that, the main five Feng Shui elements are also derived from Feng Shui. When doing a Feng Shui analysis, the Compass and the Ba-Gua are used. The Ba-Gua is a grid that is created in the shape of an octagon.

This grid has symbols of the I Ching. In fact, Feng Shui is based on this premise. In order for you to connect the areas of your home with Feng Shui, you need to understand the concept of Ba-Gua.

The compass is also known as "lo-pan", works to gain additional information about a facility. The magnetic needle is surrounded by concentric rings that are strategically placed. The word "lo" means everything and "pan" means bowl. Lo-pan is used to open the mysteries of the universe.

When learning Feng Shui, you have to start off at the basic level in order for you to understand the entire process. After you had a good understanding Feng Shui on the basic level, you will get phenomenal results. The results will affect how you perceive Feng Shui. You will want to use it on a regular basis in your home and your business.

When engaged with Feng Shui, you will need cures in order to have a better life. There are different things that can be used to achieve this. Here are five of them:

Aquariums

Fountains

Crystals

Colors

Clocks

2. Methods Of Feng Shui

Some of the methods are easy to use; however, when it comes to the main part of it, it can take a while, like several years to get the hang of it. Learning Feng Shui is not as easy as people may think it to be.

For this type of setting, you should always start from the beginning with the basics, then move your way up. It makes it easy for you and others to follow along. Then you can make gradual steps to the advances phases of Feng Shui. To get you started, here are some things that you can implement:

Air and light of good quality – You should have this in your home in order to master the Feng Shui principles. You can benefit from having good Chi when you incorporate both of them.

In order to operate this principle, it's a good idea to allow natural light into your home. The windows should be open on a frequent basis. If you're a plant lover, invest in some air purifying plants for Feng Shui.

Ba-Gua – Use the compass to activate the energy map in your home. When you connect with your Ba-Gua, you will find out which areas or rooms in your home are connected with the Feng Shui concept.

Get rid of clutter – You should discard everything that doesn't mean anything to you or reminds you of bad events or feelings in your life. If you have a lot of clutter, all of it can't be removed overnight.

After it's done, you will feel like a heavy burden has been removed from your shoulders. This is a very important thing to do because you will have a release. It will also be easier for you to move to the next phase.

Five Elements – Get familiar with the five elements of Feng Shui. For certain areas, some elements will need to be stronger. This depends on what you're trying to attract in your life. It also depends on what area of your home you're looking to implement Feng Shui.

Birth Element – Wood and Fire are considered elements and along with that you will need a color to correspond with the elements. In addition to that, you will need to incorporate shapes to match the element and color for Feng Shui.

3. The Five Elements Of Feng Shui

The principle of five elements is important to the concept of Feng Shui. They work in certain ways in accordance with the rotation of the Productive and Destructive Cycles. All five of the elements correspond with a certain color. Some of the elements will use more than one color. The best way to utilize these elements is to open your space to more happiness.

Here are the five elements and their corresponding colors:

Wood – Represents and provides energy for health and vitality; it also represents abundance and is considered a cure for wealth and prosperity. This element resides in the East and Southeast areas of your space. The Wood Element is also good for use in the South. The Wood Element colors are brown and green.

Fire – Represents high energy and passion; it provides energy to things that are career related. It will also provide assistance to have you recognized in your achievements. This element resides in the South, Northeast and Southwest areas of your space. The Fire Element colors are Red, Orange, Purple, Pink and Strong Yellow.

Water – Represents easiness, abundance and freshness; it also represents calm and purity. Water represents abundance and is considered a cure for Feng Shui. It can be used in the North, East and Southeast areas of your space. The Water Element colors are blue and black.

Earth – Represents being stable and nourishment; it also represents protection for your relationships. It can be used in the Northeast, Southeast and Center areas of your space. The Earth Element colors are beige and yellow.

Metal – Represents being precise and clear; it also represents exactness and being efficient. You can live with clarity and light.

It can be used in the West, North and Northwest areas of your space. The Metal Element is ideal for your home or business. The Metal Element colors are white and gray.

The Productive and Destructive cycles control the five elements of Feng Shui. Wood is part of the Productive Cycle that is produced by the Element Water. The Cycle continues with the creation of Fire, Earth, Metal and last but not least, Water, in that order. The Cycle does not stop and complement each other. They also maintain a positive flow with one another.

Even though it's on the opposite end, the Destructive Cycle has just as much prominence as the Productive Cycle. Anything that is negative or contributes to decay is removed. This makes way for things that are positive and will help in the Feng Shui process.

With this Cycle, Wood is responsible for separating Earth. Earth in turn, soaks up Water; Water douses out Fire; Fire melts Metal; and Metal cuts up Wood. This too, is another cycle that goes around in circles and doesn't stop.

You will need to use different colors for each direction:
East and Southeast – Dominant green
South – Dominant red
Southwest – Dominant yellow
West and Northwest – Dominant white or metallic

With the directions and color schemes, alternate colors can be used for the basic ones. Blue and black can be used for the East and Southeast. Anything in the red family can be used for the Southwest and Northwest.

Anything in the yellow, beige and brown family along with any combinations can be used for the West and Northwest. White is the color used in the North because Metal creates Water. In the South, green can be used because Wood creates Fire.

The colors don't have to stand by themselves. They can be supplemented or combined with others to create powerful statements. With Feng Shui, you must keep balance and harmony. These attributes are needed in order to keep the flow of Chi in a positive format.

Yang energy comes from the Element of Fire. It is represented by the color red. Other things that help to provide more energy are candles and lights. If you want more intimacy as far as being close is concerned, Earth energy would be needed. Things that contribute to earth energy can help your marriage in a positive way. They can also help you in different relationships.

You can use things like crystals and ceramics, things made from earthenware to enhance this. Since Metal is created by Earth, Metal can take advantage of the benefits. Metal is also one of the Yang Elements that happens to have a positive effect. Metal is also responsible for creating Water. This can help with the Chi flow.

With Water being a part of the Chi flow, the flow doesn't stop. Water helps to have Chi flowing in different areas of life. With Feng Shui, flowing water is considered to be quiet and relaxing. You can use it to implement energy in your home.

If you are looking to advance or start your career, water can be used for that purpose. It also represents wealth and prosperity. A good thing to implement for this would be an aquarium or a water fountain. This can have positive vibes in certain areas of your home. One place that water is not recommended for is the bedroom.

The Wood Element also connects with your home and garden. You can place wooden objects in certain areas in order to obtain more wealth. They can be placed near plants and flowers. Another thing that can increase wealth is installing a wooden bench in the area of your garden that is designated for Wealth.

4. The Colors Of Feng Shui

Black

Black is the color of mystery. It also provides protection. It symbolizes nighttime when it gets dark, and it also represents an empty space. Even with that, it provides intensity to any area. If it is used often, it can translate into a heavy atmosphere. Black is also used to provide strength.

This color can be used in the East, North and Southeast. It should not be used in the South. It can be used in a child's bedroom, but not a lot. It can also be used in the common areas of your home.

If you're trying to attract career opportunities, it can be used in the North area of anyone's space. Black can be combined with white to be used on furniture.

Brown

The color brown is used in the East, Southeast and the South. The energy from this color provides plenty of nourishment. It can be associated with different foods and drinks, such as chocolate and coffee.

Brown can also be used for the common areas of your home. You shouldn't use much of the color Brown for a child's bedroom or the Southwest area. If there is too much of the color in an area, it may cause people not to take a step forward.

Green

This color represents revival and a fresh start. Green provides nourishment and keeps peace in your life. When incorporated with Feng Shui, you should use different versions of green, instead of just one.

You can use plants that have fresh foliage. Green is also known to provide healing. It can be used more so in the South, East and Southeast areas.

There are different versions of this color that can be used in Feng Shui.

Red

When the colors for Feng Shui are used in the right format, your environment will be the recipient of good Feng Shui energy. The color red contributes to the Fire Element to provide energy.

Fire can be considered as a creative aspect and a destructive aspect. Fire is a symbol for sun and life and energy that comes from it. With this Element in your home, you can experience happiness and a desire to be sexually fulfilled.

Red also represents passion and celebration. The Chinese use the color red for happiness and luck. In India, the color red is use for marriage and weddings, and in the West, the color red stands for romance and courage. When people decorate, the color red is used for richness. Careful consideration has to be implemented not to use too much red. Otherwise, it can provoke anger and excessive stimulation.

With Feng Shui, red can be used in children's bedrooms with caution. It can also be used in the common areas of the home, such as the dining and living rooms and the kitchen area.

In the East, Southeast, West and Northwest areas of your home, you can use the color red, but you are limited to how much you should use. Red is a perfect candidate to use in the South.

Orange

Orange has been nicknamed the "social" color. Orange is responsible for providing the energy from Feng Shui to engage in spirited conversations and to have good feelings in your home. When the winter season approaches, it can be a reminder of the summer season. Log fires also come into play with the color of orange.

Just like red represents fire, so does orange. It is not a good color for the areas of the West and Northwest. In addition to that, this color should not be seen in the East and Southeast.

These areas are controlled by other elements of Feng Shui.

Orange can be used for the common areas, such as the living and dining rooms, kitchen, and anywhere else where the environment can have action and lots of energy. It's a good idea to have some Feng Shui products or accessories.

Since orange is considered a soft and warm color, it is easy to incorporate with Feng Shui. It is a beautiful sight to see as a sunset. It enhances the rooms and makes them stand out.

Purple

Don't overuse the color purple. This color is very strong, and has a relationship with the spirit. It is not recommended for use on the wall. It can however, be used in a space where meditation is taking place. If you use this color at home, be very moderate about using it. You can use lighter colors. It can be used in the East South and West areas, with limitations.

A good way for the color purple to be implemented is to use the Feng Shui crystal Amethyst.

Pink

The color of love is pink. It can also be used to keep the energy calm. It also works to quiet the heart and provide it with lots of love. This color is used mostly in the Southwest area. It also is in line with marriage. When decorating, a soft pink is used. When there is hot and heavy energy, hot pink is used.

Pink is great to use for a bedroom of a little girl; what little girl wouldn't want that color? Ok, there may be some, but they're probably few and far between. There are several common combinations of pink that include pink and black and pink and green. Pink and green represents activity. Pink and black represents a retro style.

With Feng Shui, rose quartz crystals can be used for love. The crystals are a soft pink that soothes the soul.

Yellow

The color yellow reminds people of the sun. It can brighten up any space and provides an inviting atmosphere. You have many choices to choose from when it comes to yellow. This color is a better choice for a child's bedroom and the family room.

If you have a dull looking room, using the color yellow will provide it with lots of light. It provides the Fire Element, but in a softer format than the color Red does. It is easier to deal with on a larger scale. Yellow can also be used to provide self-esteem. If you use hot yellow, don't use too much of it. Yellow can be used in the East and Southeast areas.

Gray

Gray is usually considered as a dull color that doesn't have much life. However, there is a shade of gray (noble gray) that is considered a little more upbeat than the regular color. Gray is used in the West, Northwest and North areas of Ba-Gua.

It should not be used too much in the East and Southeast. Wood is the dominant Element in those areas. Believe it or not, gray can provide Feng Shui energy into most of the common areas in your home.

It can provide a clear focus to any space in your home. Gray also represents the energy of the Metal Element.

White

The color white represents Yoga rituals. With Feng Shui, it stands for quietness and innocence. It also stands for beginnings and endings. It has a clean and fresh focus. It can be used for Feng Shui purposes anywhere in your home.

In the East and Southeast, it's not a good idea to use all white. You can use other colors to blend in with it.

You can have white space in your bathroom or mediation room. This will help with healing in your home. It can also provide possibilities never explored before along with a promising future.

Blue

Blue represents the clear skies and waters. It can be used in the East and Southeast of anyone's space. Since blue is connected with Water, the energy is responsible for supplying nourishment to the Wood Element. It can also be use for decoration or art.

Blue can also be used as a color for ceilings. It's been note that students did better in their studies when they have a blue ceiling.

For harmony, a light blue color would work well. For peace and quiet, a dark blue color would work better. A deep blue color can be implemented in your bedroom to help to get to sleep.

For the South, West and Northwest areas, deep blue should not be utilized much. Blue and white colors can be combined to provide energy.

5. Introduction On Creating A Happy Home With Feng Shui

The areas that are incorporated with Feng Shui are built to have energy in mind. There is always energy around us that continues to circulate every minute of the day. You can do the same thing at your home. Incorporating the principles of Feng Shui can help you to have a healthy and happy home.

When you do this, expect the atmosphere to change. When people come to visit, they will feel happier to be in your home and in your presence. When they are happy, you will be happy. If you were pessimistic before, your demeanor will change to the opposite. As long as you keep the exchange of positive energy flowing, you will be able to relish in type of environment.

Get familiar with certain areas of your home. The more you are aware about what the areas are comprised of, the more success you will have of incorporating those areas with the principles of Feng Shui. With this, you will be able to transfer this to other areas of your life, including your relationships with family members and friends.

Let's look at some things that can advance and enhance this:

You should have a connection to your home. Examine the areas of your home and determine which parts do not line up with the Feng Shui principles. Whatever doesn't line up will eventually have a detrimental effect in your life. It will also cause you not to have as much energy in those areas.

Don't overreact if your home or areas in it are not responding the way you would like them to. An example would be if you have a basement in your home that is in need of painting, don't get upset because it hasn't been painted.

Create some Feng Shui instructions for yourself so that you can go ahead and get the work done. Don't get angry or agitated as you compile them. Just think of it as something that has to be done.

There will be time when you can let out your emotions, but don't allow them to be a hindrance for your assignment.

When you remove clutter from your home, you are able to provide positive and fresh energy. Your home will also be healthier as a result. Having clutter represents confusion and indecisiveness.

That can prove to be a negative thing for you if you're working to incorporate Feng Shui in your life. Once the clutter is gone, you will have a sense of relief and whatever stress you had will be gone. This can also help you to have a healthier peace of mind.

Another thing that some people feel they are lacking in is relationships, whether it's a marriage, friendship, or relationship with your children, siblings, parents or other relatives. How does this work in the equation? Well, having positive relationships can provide you with more energy.

People want to feel that someone cares about their well-being. Maintaining any kind of relationship takes work and it doesn't happen overnight. There are some that are healthy, and others are just falling by the wayside.

In regard to your home, there are some ways that can help you to keep your relationships fresh and positive:

Change the format of your furniture. If you have enough room, move it around to another angle or another wall. Don't keep any furniture, such as a couch, bed, table or chairs in the same format every year. It starts to become monotonous. Moving your furniture around can help provide more energy in that area.

Whatever area of your house it is, focus on providing additional energy that is positive. You can do that by having fresh fruits, fresh flowers, or anything that is fresh and stands out.

Your bedrooms, bathrooms and closets should be clutter free. They should be areas that people wouldn't mind looking at if you were showing your house to someone.

Having a television in your bedroom is not necessarily a good idea. It can be a distraction from your actual purpose.

Have pictures of you and your loved ones in a positive format.

Don't crowd people and don't allow them to crowd you. Everyone needs space and time for themselves.

Listen to music that is relaxing and soothes the soul. Certain types of music can provide great energy in the right environment.

6. Incorporating Feng Shui If Your Home Is In A Cul-de-sac

Feng Shui may not operate too well when your home is located in a cul-de-sac. However, that's not speaking for all of the homes in that curved area. There are some homes that have good flow of energy that still may not get the flow of Chi coming through.

Here are some explanations as to why a cul-de-sac home may not receive the proper flow of Feng Shui that it should:

When a home is in a cul-de-sac, there is a back and forth movement of shared energy between homes of three or more. The energy within those homes wavers and can't be still. This causes less energy to flow through; of course, this hinges on the homes in that particular cul-de-sac.

Here are some ways that the Feng Shui cul-de-sac issue can be solved:

The landscaping should be neat and provide energy. The homes should also have a quality backing that is sturdy and will hold up. Evergreens can also be installed in the back of the home.

The walkway to the front of the home should be curved. Also in the front of the home, plant some greens and decorate with colorful rocks. At least the person coming to visit will have something to look at as they step to the front of your home.

Install a fountain or moving water outside of your home. Or you could install a birdbath. With Feng Shui, the fountain or birdbath should be installed in the direction that your home is facing. In addition to that, the water flow should be flowing in the same direction.

Your front door may need to be a certain color. If your door is facing North, you may want to opt for a black or blue color for the door. Since that represents calm, you don't have to concern yourself with a lot of confusion in and around your home.

Just remember that each home is different, so there may be some homes within a particular cul-de-sac that may have plenty of energy for Feng Shui. There may be some outside of that area that do not have that energy. There are several factors that play into this scenario.

Why You Should Not Use Direct Alignment For The Doors In Your Home

When using Feng Shui, it's important that the doors inside and outside the door are covered. A lot of people are concerned that this part of the home seems to be on the backburner. However, it is as important, if not more than the rest of the spaces in the home. Direct alignment of more than one door is not proper. It can contribute to bad Feng Shui.

Even though the concept of Feng Shui is to have a balance with the energy flow in your home, having a direct alignment with more than one door cannot work. The quality of energy flow from Feng Shui is subject to decrease.

One area where you do not want to do this is with the front and the back door. The majority of the energy from the good Feng Shui is from the front door. If those two doors are aligned, the energy can travel through the back door. This is not good because the energy from the good Feng Shui need to permeate throughout your home. Nourishment is also needed.

Take note of what kind of energy is being created in your home. If it's not enough, see what you can do to create more energy for more good Feng Shui. However, if you door have doors in your home that are directly aligned with each other, there are some things that you can do to remedy that situation:

In order for you to change the way the doors are situated, you may have to change the color of one of the doors. After the color change, the relationship will be different, one of the doors will have more strength than the other.

Where the energy is, you can place a small round table there. The energy will be directed elsewhere and the energy will slow down. For improvement, add a vase or similar container with fresh flowers. Doing this will give more credence to the energy.

If you don't want use fresh flowers, get a plant with a pot. Having a plant will also send the energy in another direction.

The purpose in doing these things is to redirect the energy in another direction. Don't forget to incorporate Chi and send the water flow in another direction. It's important to keep the energy from Feng Shui flowing in your home.

7. Feng Shui For Your Kitchen

Incorporating Feng Shui for your kitchen will take some surveying. You have to look at how it is placed within the home. The kitchen is usually located adjacent to the backyard of the home. There's a good reason for that.

From a visual standpoint, if the kitchen was near or at the front, it could pose a mindset of issues with eating and nutrition. Having it in the front of the home could mean that you may be tempted to eat every time you enter. It would be just as bad if you have guests coming to visit. The first thing they would want to do is eat.

However, if your home is set up like this, you can do something about it. You could purchase a curtain and install in the area of the kitchen entryway. Or, you could have French doors measured to install in that area. Another idea you could implement is to have something that will peak their interest. This can cause a distraction on the real focus (the kitchen).

If you're cooking, you should have an eye on the entryway of the kitchen. There are kitchen where the stove is facing the wall. To implement to the Feng Shui method, people that are cooking can put a mirror over the stove.

For newer homes, builders are now including islands that sit in the middle of the kitchen area. This would be a good addition to the Feng Shui concept. When the island is strategically placed in the middle, the person that's cooking can see what's going on in another area.

When it's set up this way, they can still be involved with what's happening in a nearby area, along with continue to cook meals.

This type of kitchen setup is inviting because it allows other people to come in and help cook. The original person that was doing all of the cooking won't feel slighted. It can make for a greater camaraderie and relationship bonding.

In Feng Shui, the stove is the symbol of health and wealth. All of the burners should be used equally by doing rotations. Don't use one or two burners and leave the rest unused. Using all four in equal rotation can cause you to receive money from more than one source.

It has been noted that with the older model stoves, those are actually better because they incorporate the Feng Shui method of slowing down. Take a good look at what's going on and what you're doing.

While microwaving food may be quick and convenient, in the interim you may still feel rushed. People that faithfully practice the Feng Shui method do not like to use microwaves due to lots of radiation.

The kitchen should be one of the cleanest areas in the home. It should also be clutter-free. If you have anything that is not working properly or not working at all, it should be discarded. Having something that doesn't work or doesn't work properly defeats the purpose and the principles of Feng Shui.

You can also use different design methods and patterns from the Feng Shui concept. The methods most used are a Shaker style concept, contemporary with solid colors and wood grains and a wealthy look that comes with carvings and other related items.

The kitchen should have adequate lighting and using different types. There should be enough space to move around. The more space you have, the better. If it means you have to move machines and appliances to create more space, then so be it.

You don't need a lot of kitchen equipment or utensils in front of you. Use only the things that you're going to cook with. When you're finished with those items, you can place them in the sink to be washed later. At least they will be out of the way.

To increase the energy in the kitchen, you may want to have some fruit, flowers or a plant on the table. This will also brighten up the kitchen to make it look more inviting. Cooking in the kitchen is where the heart is. You want to have a place where people can come and enjoy your company.

8. Create Wealth And Abundance Using Feng Shui In Your Bathroom

A bathroom is one of the places where you can incorporation Feng Shui for the purpose of wealth. There are different strategies that you can use to accomplish this.

Color – From the different elements, you can use different colors to achieve your goal of attracting wealth from using Feng Shui. With Wood, you should use brown and green; with Water, use blue and black; with Earth, you can use colors in the yellow and brown collection, such as light yellow or light beige.

Crystals – You can purchase Feng Shui crystals to use. Mix them up using amethyst, citrine, rose quartz and others in the crystal family. This combination can create a wealth cure in Feng Shui.

Bamboo – Another Feng Shui cure for wealth and abundance is to have 8 stalks of Lucky Bamboo. This cure is used by a lot of people and they can be found in plenty of floral retailers.

On the other hand, there are people that don't take care of them like they should. Bamboo is very easy to maintain, yet people don't make an effort to do that. It represents tranquility and relaxation. All five elements of Feng Shui have a part to play in the bamboo plant.

Atmosphere – Decorate your bathroom so that it looks like a spa. A spa is a place where you go to relax. Having a massage will take away all of the cares in the world. All you'll be thinking about is having a peace of mind

Clutter – Remove any excess or clutter that doesn't need to be there. If you have items that have expired, get rid of them. If there are things that you haven't used in a long time, get rid of those also. You want to have things in your bathroom that represent positive energy. It's also important that the lighting is good as well.

Meaning of wealth – Whatever wealth means to you, put it in the bathroom. It could be a picture, a poem or some quote that will remind you of wealth.

Toilet seat – The toilet seat should remain down when not in use. This will show that the energy will be maintained and not spread out everywhere outside of that area.

9. Implementing Mirrors With The Concept Of Feng Shui

Mirrors are generally used as a reflection. People use them to look themselves. With Feng Shui, they help to bring in water. They are also used to pull in the Chi method in addition to widening space. Mirrors can change the way energy flows in a certain area. They are good for bringing peace and a fresh new outlook on life.

With Feng Shui, three types of mirrors are used. Here's a brief synopsis of them:

Convex – These mirrors are considered to represent protection. They are the eyes and ears and most of the time, are utilized apart from Feng Shui. They can also be used within the concept, but they have to be framed a certain way.

Concave – Most of the time, these mirrors are not used inside Feng Shui. The reflection from the mirrors is a smaller version that is turned upside-down.

Typical – Depending on the shape and the frame, it represents a certain Feng Shui cure. They are usually placed in the Southwest portion of your area.

There's also the Ba-Gua Mirror, which is separate from the three mirrors mentioned above. It is very powerful and for the most part, people don't use it correctly. It is only made for outdoors, not indoors. If you're not feeling the right kind of energy in your home or business, then this type of mirror will come in handy for you. This mirror is not to be used for decoration.

The Ba-Gua mirror is found in concave and convex formats. The Ba-Gua itself is made from wood and there is a choice of green, red or gold.

The Ba-Gua mirror is good to use if you need to protect yourself from harm or danger, such as attacks against you or if there are people out to harm you.

You should consult with a person that is knowledgeable in Feng Shui in order that it is placed in the right area. Most times, it is placed above the main entrance to your home. One place that it should not be placed at is in the living room.

10. Feng Shui In Your Bedroom To Enhance Your Love Life

In order to have a positive, intimate relationship with your mate, you need a good feng shui bedroom. Both of you will be able to spend time renewing yourselves, minus having to deal with a lot of unnecessary stuff.

Only one significant piece of furniture should be placed in your bedroom and that's the bed. You have to have something to sleep on. Get something simple like a wood bed frame along with a natural mattress. The sheets that you sleep under should be made from cotton of the best quality or close. Do not have any electronics except things like a clock.

Part of the Yin culture includes sleeping. It is important that the bedroom is situated at the back of your home where there is minimal activity. Your bedroom should look warm and inviting. After all, it is where you share intimate and tender moments alone with each other.

Here are some more Feng Shui suggestions you can use for your bedroom:

The bedroom should not be placed over the garage. This is where you can incorporate low energy and issues with your health. Also, electrical elements from the vehicle parked in the garage can mess with your electromagnetic system.

Try not to use items that run on electricity in the bedroom. These items can provoke a high electrical charge.

If possible, the bedroom should not be anywhere the kitchen, bathroom, living room or children's bedroom.

To keep the flames going in your sex and love life, there should always be fresh energy in the bedroom. This can be implemented by using crystals, candles or essential oils.

Keeping the bedroom with good Feng Shui will help to maintain a positive flow and sensual feelings of energy. A good Feng Shui bedroom should be filled with lots of love and passion. It should also be exciting and provide relaxation.

Here are some more ways that you can create a good Feng Shui bedroom:

Don't have stale air in your bedroom. Open the window and let in some fresh air, weather permitting. You should have fresh air flowing in your bedroom. In addition to removing the majority of electrical appliances, it is not advisable to have plants in the bedroom, either.

The lighting in the bedroom should be adjustable. The easiest way to do this is to install a dimmer switch. You will be able to adjust the lights to an appropriate level. You can also use candles, but purchase those that are toxin free.

Use colors that correspond with the Feng Shui method. The colors should create a balance for the bedroom. This way, you will be assured of a positive energy flow. This will help you go to sleep better. It will also help your sexual life as well. Some colors that would work well in the bedroom include whites and chocolate brown colors.

If you're looking to add art to your bedroom, choose pieces that reflect how you look at your life and your future n a positive way. Refrain from using pieces that represent anything that is the opposite of that.

The Feng Shui procedure for your bed should be as follows: You should be able to gain access to your bed from both sides. The bed should not be parallel with the bedroom door. You can have two small tables on each side of your bed. Doing these things will help your bed and bedroom maintain a balance.

All of the doors that are connected to the bedroom should be closed. Whether it's the entry door, closet door or inside bathroom door, none of them should be ajar. This will keep the energy flow inside of the bedroom. It will also enhance your relationship with your mate.

You want to have a bedroom that will be the symbol of pleasure, intimacy and love. Using the Feng Shui method can help you do just that.

11. Feng Shui For Your Home Based Business

Believe it or not, there are many business people all over the world that use the principles of Feng Shui in their business. Many Asians believe Feng Shui is necessary in order to conduct proper business and business management. In fact, there are some famous businesspeople in the United States that are using Feng Shui and they have encountered good success in their business.

Many people have transformed themselves into entrepreneurs and having their office established in their home. This is a cost effective way to start out because there is not much overhead.

On the other side, some people that work from home find themselves somewhat perplexed because it can be difficult for them to separate their home business from their personal life and they don't have a lot of interaction with other people. However, having a home base business outweighs the challenges and frustrations that people face working at a 9 to 5 job.

If you're looking to attract wealth and abundance for your home based business using Feng Shui, here are some ways to incorporate it:

You should always sit with a solid wall behind your back. Avoid sitting with a window behind you.

You should not have a wall facing you while you're at your desk working or when you come into the office.

Wherever your wealth area is, you should have the office equipment placed there.

In order for Chi to flow with harmony, place the tables and chairs in a strategic format.

Have air-purifying plants in your home office. This will help supply you with a fresh quality of air and it will also increase the amount of oxygen generated in that area.

Other than air-purifying plants, refrain from having any plants that have sharp edges, such as cactus.

The entry door to your home office should be free of obstruction. If there is obstruction, such as a table behind the door, the Chi will not operate correctly.

In order to enhance the presence of Chi, a good idea is to install a hanging crystal in your home office.

Your home office should be a good distance from your bedroom.

Your home office should be about productivity. The colors of your home office should reflect that.

The copy machine should not be near the main entry door. The heat from the copy machine can cause to Chi not to flow correctly.

If there is an empty vase near the main entry door, the Chi will find its way into the empty vase. This will be a detriment to the environment.

If you have clients that come to see you, try placing a fish tank within the wealth area. This will help you get better results and probably more clients, which in turn, means more money. You have to be careful to follow the instructions for doing this, otherwise it won't work.

In order to get Chi working properly, install a small indoor fountain in your wealth corner. This method will also help you health wise.

Keep your desks and surrounding areas clutter free. To help with this, the Chinese do not use paper trays. The concept is starting to make its way in the United States.

Pay attention to the kind of light that you are using in your home office. You should use both natural and artificial lighting.

You will not be able to function properly if you don't have enough natural light.

You should also think about getting other type of lights, such as full-spectrum lights. These lights are similar to the natural light spectrum and they have been branded as healthier to use.

There are different areas of your home office that need to be nurtured with Feng Shui. In the North area, the Water Element is used as well as Metal. In your home office, it's fine to have images with black or white frames.

The South area uses Fire for energy. You should refrain from having blue mirrors, or images of water that represent this color. The Southeast area is for images that represent prosperity and abundance. The Wood Element is used here. With this, you should refrain from Fire and Metal images.

Using these Feng Shui principles will help your business to thrive and grow in prosperity and abundance.

12. Using Feng Shui For Your Online Business

You can use Feng Shui to create harmony for your websites. Your web pages must be aligned properly. You want the visitors that come to your site to have easy navigation and access. It should be a positive experience for them.

The pages should be clean and use bright colors for the background. If you create web pages with a dark color, it can be a turnoff to those that are visiting your website. In order to start to Chi flow, you can use bold colors.

White and blue are a few that come to mind. These colors are the symbols of air and water. If you use colors that don't blend very well, your website will not be attractive. You can incorporate bad Feng Shui if it doesn't look right.

Refrain from adding things like animated graphics that take away from the essence of the website. If it has to be part of the website, then make sure it's something that looks natural.

On your website, you should have an area that displays a logo. This logo would be on every webpage that you create. Refrain from putting a lot of games and other gimmicks on your website and web pages. This can distract the visitors.

Your website should have a main menu page. All of the elements that you're putting on the website should not be lined up on one side of the screen or cluttered on both sides of the screen.

Don't make your website look so professional that no one will want to stay. Create websites that will bring harmony and a good atmosphere to the visitors. If you're going to incorporate music, use music that is relaxing. This will help to create positive Chi.

The important thing with creating websites using Feng Shui is that you want them to be simple, easy to navigate and not look rushed or cluttered. Too much stuff on it and people will turn away in a heartbeat.

Ironically, having a rushed or cluttered website can be reflective of the person themselves. It's about having a positive flow so that good Chi will continue to flow through.

13. Using Feng Shui For A Retail Business

You may want to open up a retail store. You have plenty of products, but you don't have any idea on how to attract or keep customers once they set foot in your business. You don't understand what's going on and need some assistance in this arena.

Using the principles of Feng Shui can change your situation. Here's a look at some things that you can do to change the atmosphere of your business:

You have too many things bunched together. The products are nice, but there's no sense of what goes where. Or they may be thinking, "Why is this product here when it should be somewhere else?"

You must remove some of the products and leave some space between them. Bunching them up together does nothing but cause confusion for the customer. They feel it's too much for them to look at.

Try to put the products in different categories. Then you'll see a difference when customers come in. They'll want to stay longer and look because they're not confused and frustrated with what to purchase.

The Feng Shui energy from the entry door to the back door is not flowing properly. In turn, you don't get customers or sales. The minute the customer walks in the door, they need to be drawn in by what you have.

Be clear on the products you offer and their benefits. Customers always want to know what's in it for them. After all, you're marketing to them, so why not let them know how they can benefit if they purchase?

The entry way and the front area should be more visible than the back. They will see the front of the store first before they make their way back.

Your aisles are not clear. You have things in the way that are creating obstacles for the customer. That should not be. A customer doesn't want to be squeezing through or stepping over things just to get by. Make room in the aisles for them so they'll have easy access to the products.

Some of these suggestions can be implemented for the internet as well. Conduct a survey or ask some of your customers are there things that you can make changes to with your store. You might be surprised with the answers. It's very important that you tune in to the customer's needs. Without them, there would be no business.

14. Conclusion

Whether it's to improve your health, love life or finances, Feng Shui has been incorporated as a way to do this. The method has worked for the Chinese people for many years. Since it has spread, people are curious to find out how it can help them. This e-book has provided plenty of information to get your started on your journey to abundance and other things that can enhance your life.

If you stay on the right path with this and are serious about making significant changes in your life, you will see a difference. You will be amazed at how much healthier you've become. You'll be so excited to get intimate with your mate, it'll be breathtaking. With your finances, you can have more money than you ever dreamed possible when using the Feng Shui method.

Just remember that everything won't happen overnight and that it will take time before you see a change in your life for the better.

16873364R00024

Printed in Great Britain
by Amazon